Standing in Grace

Jonathan Edwards's
A Treatise on Grace

Edited by Dr. Don Kistler

Soli Deo Gloria Publications
. . . for instruction in righteousness . . .

Soli Deo Gloria Publications
P. O. Box 451, Morgan, PA 15064
(412) 221-1901/FAX 221-1902
www.SDGbooks.com

*

Standing in Grace: Jonathan Edwards's Treatise on Grace was
first published in Edinburgh in 1865 by Alexander
Grosart, under the title *A Treatise on Grace,* and was
published as part of *Selections from the Unpublished
Writings of Jonathan Edwards.* This Soli Deo Gloria
reprint, in which spelling, grammar, and
formatting changes have been made

*

ISBN 1-57358-131-3

Library of Congress Cataloging-in-Publication Data

Edwards, Jonathan, 1703–1758.
    [Treatise on grace]
    Standing in grace: Jonathan Edwards's A treatise
        on grace/edited by Don Kistler.
        p. cm.
    ISBN 1-57358-131-3
    1. Grace (Theology) I. Kistler, Don. II. Title.
    BT761.3 .E38 2002
    234–dc21
                                    2002004051

Contents

Chapter 1

Common and saving grace differ not only in degree,
but in nature and kind

Such phrases as "common grace," and "special or
saving grace," may be understood as signifying either
diverse kinds of influence of God's Spirit on the hearts
of men, or diverse fruits and effects of that influence.
The Spirit of God is supposed sometimes to have some
influence upon the minds of men who are not true
Christians, and it is supposed that those dispositions,
frames, and exercises of their minds that are of a good
tendency, but are common to them with the saints, are
in some respect owing to some influence or assistance
of God's Spirit. But as there are some things in the
hearts of true Christians that are peculiar to them, and
that are more excellent than anything that is to be
found in others, so it is supposed that there is an operation of the Spirit of God that is different, and that the
value which distinguishes them is owing to a higher
influence and assistance than the virtues of others. So
sometimes the phrase "common grace" is used to signify that kind of action or influence of the Spirit of
God to which are owing those religious or moral attainments that are common to both saints and sinners, and
so signifies as much as common assistance; and sometimes those moral or religious attainments themselves

that are the fruits of this assistance are intended. So likewise the phrase "special or saving grace" is sometimes used to signify that peculiar kind or degree of separation or influence of God's Spirit, whence saving actions and attainments arise in the godly, or (which is the same thing) special and saving assistance; or else to signify that distinguishing saving virtue itself which is the fruit of this assistance. These phrases are more frequently understood in the latter sense, that is, not for common and special assistance, but for common and special (or saving) virtue, which is the fruit of that assistance, and so I would be understood by these phrases in this discourse.

Special or saving grace in this sense is not only different from common grace in degree, but entirely diverse in nature and kind; and natural men not only do not have a sufficient degree of virtue to be saints, but they have no degree of that grace that is in godly men—these are the things I have now to show.

This is evident by what Christ says in John 3:6, where Christ, speaking of regeneration, says, "That which is born of the flesh is flesh, and that which is born of the Spirit is spirit." Now, whatever Christ intends by the terms "flesh" and "spirit" in the words, yet this much is manifest and undeniable, that Christ here intends to show Nicodemus the necessity of a new birth, or another birth than his natural birth; and that, from this argument a man who has been the subject of the first birth only has nothing of that in his heart which he must have in order to enter into the kingdom. He has nothing at all of that which Christ calls "spirit," whatever that is. All that a man has who has only been the subject of a natural birth doesn't go beyond that which

Christ calls "flesh," for however it may be refined and exalted, yet it cannot be raised above flesh. It is plain that by "flesh" and "spirit" Christ here intends two things that are entirely different in nature, which cannot be one from the other. A man cannot have anything of a nature superior to flesh who is not born again, and therefore we must be born again. That by flesh and spirit are intended certain moral principles, natures, or qualities, entirely different and opposite in their nature one to another, is manifest from other texts, particularly Galatians 5:17: "For the flesh lusteth against the spirit, and the spirit against the flesh; and they are contrary the one to the other; so that ye cannot do the things which ye would." Verse 19: "Now the works of the flesh are manifest, which are these: adultery, fornication," and so on. Verse 22: "But the fruit of the Spirit is love, joy, peace. . . ." Galatians 6:8: "For he that soweth to the flesh shall of the flesh reap corruption; but he that soweth to the Spirit shall of the Spirit reap life everlasting." Romans 8:6: "For to be carnally minded is death, but to be spiritually minded is life and peace." 1 Corinthians 3:1: "And I, brethren, could not speak unto you as unto spiritual, but as unto carnal, even as unto babes in Christ." So that it is manifest by this that men who have been the subjects of the first birth only have no degree of that moral principle or quality that those who are newly born have, whereby they have a title to the kingdom of heaven. This principle or quality comes out then in no other way than by birth; and the birth that it must come by is not, cannot be, the first birth, but it must be a new birth. If men who have no title to the kingdom of heaven could have something of the Spirit as well as flesh, then

Christ's argument would be false. It is plain by Christ's reasoning that those who are not in a state of salvation cannot have these two opposite principles in their hearts together, some flesh and some spirit, lusting one against the other as the godly have, but that they have flesh only.

The only principle in those who are savingly converted whence gracious acts flow in the language of Scripture is called "the spirit," and is set in opposition to "the flesh." This is that which others not only do not have a sufficient degree of, but have nothing at all of; this is further manifest because the Scriptures assert both. It negatively asserts that those who do not have the Spirit are not Christ's in Romans 8:9: "But ye are not in the flesh but in the Spirit, if so be that the Spirit of God dwell in you. Now if any man have not the Spirit of Christ, he is none of His." And it also asserts positively that those who have the Spirit are His. 1 John 3:24: "Hereby we know that He abideth in us by the Spirit which He hath given us." And our having the Spirit of God dwelling in our hearts is mentioned as a certain sign that persons are entitled to heaven, and is called the earnest of the future inheritance (2 Corinthians 1:22 and 5:5; Ephesians 1:14), which it would not be if others who had no title to the inheritance might have some of it dwelling in them.

Yea, that those who are not true saints have nothing of the Spirit, no part nor portion of it, is still more evident because not only a having any particular motion of the spirit, but a being of the Spirit is given as a sure sign of being in Christ. 1 John 4:13: "Hereby know we that we dwell in Him, and He in us, because He hath given us of His Spirit." If those who are not true saints have any degree of that spiritual principle, then though they have not so much, yet they have it, and so that would be no sign that a person is in Christ. If those who do not have a saving interest in Christ have nothing of the Spirit, then they have nothing, no degree of those graces that are the fruits of the Spirit mentioned in Galatians 5:22–23: "But the fruit of the Spirit is love, joy, peace, longsuffering, gentleness, goodness, faith, meekness, temperance." Those fruits are here mentioned with that very design, that we may know whether we have the Spirit or not.

Those who are not true saints, and are not in a state of salvation, not only do not have so much of that holy nature and divine principle that is in the hearts of the saints, but they do not partake of it, because being "partakers of the divine nature" is spoken of as the peculiar privilege of true saints (2 Peter 1:4). It is evident that it is the true saints that the apostle is there speaking of. The words in this verse with the foregoing are these: "According as His divine power hath given to us all things that pertain to life and godliness, through the knowledge of Him that hath called us to glory and virtue; whereby are given to us exceeding great and precious promises; that by these ye might be partakers of the divine nature; having escaped the corruption that is in the world through lust." The "divine nature" and "lust" are evidently here spoken of as two opposite principles in man. Those who are in the world, and who are the men of the world, have only the latter principle; but to be partakers of the divine nature is spoken of as peculiar to them who are distinguished and separated from the world by the free and sovereign grace of God giving them all things that pertain to life and godliness, giving the knowledge of Him, calling them to glory and virtue, and giving them the exceeding great and precious promises of the gospel, and who have escaped the corruption of the world of wicked men. And being partakers of the divine nature is spoken of not only as peculiar to the saints, but as one of the highest privileges of the saints.

That those who do not have a saving interest in Christ have no degree of that relish and sense of spiritual things, or things of the Spirit, of their divine truth and excellency which a true saint has, is evident from 1 Corinthians 2:14: "The natural man receiveth not the things of the Spirit of God, for they are foolishness unto him, neither can he know them because they are spiritually discerned." A natural man is here set in opposition to a spiritual one, or one who has the Spirit, as appears by the foregoing and following verses. Such persons we have shown already the Scripture declares all true saints to be, and none other. Therefore, by natural men are meant those who do not have the Spirit of Christ and are none of His, and are the subjects of no other than the natural birth. But here we are plainly taught that a natural man is perfectly destitute of any sense, perception, or discerning of those things of the Spirit. We are taught that by the words "he neither does nor can know them, or discern them." So far from this they are "foolishness unto him." He is a perfect stranger, so that he does not know what the talk of such things means; they are words without meaning to him; he knows nothing of the matter any more than a blind man knows of colors.

Hence it will follow that the sense of things of religion that a natural man has is not only not to the same degree, but nothing of the same nature with that which a true saint has. And besides, if a natural person has the fruit of the Spirit which is of the same kind with what a spiritual person has, then he experiences within himself the things of the Spirit of God; and how then can he be said to be such a stranger to them and have no perception or discerning of them?

The reason natural men have no knowledge of spiritual things is because they have nothing of the Spirit of God dwelling in them. This is evident by the context; for there we are told that it is by the Spirit that these things are taught (verses 10–12); and godly persons in the next verse are called spiritual because they have the Spirit dwelling in them. Hereby the sense again is confirmed, for natural men are in no degree spiritual; they have only nature and no Spirit. If they had anything of the Spirit, though not in so great a degree as the godly, yet they would be taught spiritual things, or things of the Spirit, in proportion to the measure of the Spirit that they had. The Spirit who searches all things would teach them in some measure. There would not be so great a difference that the one could perceive nothing of them, and that they should be foolishness to them, while to the other they appear divinely and remarkably wise and excellent, as they are spoken of in the context (verses 6–9)—and as such the apostle speaks here of discerning them.

The reason why natural men have no knowledge or perception of spiritual things is because they have none of the anointing spoken of in 1 John 2:27: "The anointing which ye have received of Him abideth in you, and you need not that any man teach you." This anointing is evidently spoken of here as a thing pecu-

liar to true saints. Ungodly men never had any degree
of that holy oil poured upon them, and therefore have
no discerning of spiritual things. Therefore none of
that sense that natural men have of things of religion
is of the same nature with what the godly have; to these
they are totally blind. Therefore, in conversion, the eyes
of the blind are opened. The world is wholly unac-
quainted with the Spirit of God, as appears from John
14:17, where we read about "the Spirit of truth whom
the world cannot receive, because it knoweth Him not."

That those who are not true saints and are not in a
state of salvation have no charity is plainly implied in
the beginning of 1 Corinthians 13. Therefore they have
no degree of that kind of grace, disposition, or
affection, that is so called. So Christ elsewhere reproves
the Pharisees, those high pretenders to religion among
the Jews, that they did not have the love of God in them
(John 5:42).

That those who are not true saints have no degree of
that grace which the saints have is evident because they
have no communion or fellowship with Christ. If those
who are not true saints partake of any of that Spirit,
those holy inclinations and affections, and gracious
acts of soul that the godly have from the indwelling of
the Spirit of Christ, then they would have communion
with Christ. The communion of saints with Christ certainly very much consists in that receiving of His fullness and partaking of His grace spoken of in John 1:16:
"Of His fullness have all we received, and grace for
grace," and in partaking of that Spirit which God gives
(not by measure) unto Him. Partaking of Christ's holiness and grace, His nature, inclinations, tendencies,
love and desires, comforts and delights, must be to have

communion with Christ. Yes, a believer's communion with the Father and the Son mainly consists in his partaking of the Holy Ghost, as appears from 2 Corinthians 13:14: "The grace of the Lord Jesus Christ, and the love of God, and the communion of the Holy Ghost."

But that unbelievers have no fellowship or communion with Christ appears, first, because they are not united to Christ; they are not in Christ. For the Scripture is very plain and evident that those who are in Christ are actually in a state of salvation, and are justified, sanctified, accepted of Christ, and shall be saved. Philippians 3:8–9: "Yea, doubtless, and I count all things but loss for the excellency of the knowledge of Christ Jesus my Lord; for whom I have suffered the loss of all things, and do count them but dung, that I may win Christ and be found in Him." 2 Corinthians 5:17: "If any man be in Christ, he is a new creature; old things are passed away; behold, all things are become new." 1 John 2:5: "But whoso keepeth His Word, in him verily is the love of God perfected; hereby know we that we are in Him"; and 3:24: "He that keepeth His commandments dwelleth in Him, and He in him; and hereby we know that He abideth in us, by the Spirit which He hath given us."

But those who are not in Christ, and are not united to Him, can have no degree of communion with Him; for there is no communion without union. The members can have no communion with the head, or participation of its life and health, unless they are united to it. The branch must be united with the vine, otherwise there can be no communication from the vine to it, nor any partaking of any degree of its sap, life, or influence. So without the union of the wife to the husband, she can have no communion in his goods.

Second, the Scripture more directly teaches that it is only true saints who have communion with Christ; particularly this is most evidently spoken of as what belongs to the saints, and to them only in 1 John 1:3: "That which we have seen and heard declare we unto you, that ye also may have fellowship with us; and truly our fellowship is with the Father, and with His Son Jesus Christ." Verses 6–7: "If we say that we have fellowship with Him and walk in darkness, we lie, and do not the truth; but if we walk in the light, as He is in the light, we have fellowship one with another, and the blood of Jesus Christ His Son cleanseth us from all sin." 1 Corinthians 1:9: "God is faithful, by whom ye were called unto the fellowship of His Son Christ Jesus our Lord."

The Scripture speaks of the actual being of a truly holy and gracious principle in the heart as inconsistent with a man's being a sinner or a wicked man. 1 John 3:9: "Whosoever is born of God doth not commit sin; for His seed remaineth in him; and he cannot sin because he is born of God." Here it is needless to dispute what is intended by this seed, whether it is a principle of true virtue and a holy nature in the soul, or whether it is the Word of God as the cause of that virtue. For let us understand it in either sense, it comes to much the same thing in the present argument; for if by the seed is meant the Word of God, yet when it is spoken of as abiding in him who is born again, it must be intended, with respect to its effect, as a holy principle in his heart; for the Word of God does not abide in one who is born again more than another in any other way than in its effect. The Word of God abides in the heart of a regenerate person as a holy seed, a divine principle there, though it may be but as a seed, a small thing. The seed is a very small part of the plant, and is its first principle. It may be in the heart as a grain of mustard seed, may be hidden, and seem to be in a great measure buried in the earth, yet it is inconsistent with wickedness. The smallest degrees and first principles of a divine and holy nature and disposition are inconsistent with a state of sin; whence it is said, "he cannot sin." There is no need here of a critical inquiry into the import of that expression; for doubtless so much at least is implied through this: "His seed being in him" is inconsistent with his being a sinner or a wicked man. So the heavenly plant of true holiness cannot be in the heart of a sinner, no, so much as in its first principle.

This is confirmed by the things that conversion is represented by in the Scriptures, particularly its being represented as a work of creation. When God creates, He does not merely establish and perfect the things which were made before, but makes wholly and immediately something entirely new, either out of nothing, or out of that which was perfectly void of any such nature, as when He made man of the dust of the earth. The things that are seen are not made of things that appear. Saving grace in man is said to be the new man or a new creature, and corrupt nature the old man. If the nature that is in the heart of a godly man is not different in its nature and kind from all that went before, then the man might possibly have had the same things a year before, and from time to time from the beginning of his life, but only not quite to the same degree. How then is grace in the new man or the new creature?

Again, conversion is often compared to a resurrection. Wicked men are said to be dead, but when they are converted they are represented as being, by God's mighty and effectual power, raised from the dead. Now there is no medium point between being dead and alive. He who is dead has no degree of life; he who has the least degree of life in him is alive. When a man is raised from the dead, life is not only in a greater degree, but it is all new.

The same is manifested by conversion being represented as a new birth, or as regeneration. Generation is not only perfecting what is old, but it is begetting from the new. The nature and life that is then received has then its beginning; it receives its first principles.

Again, conversion in Scripture is represented as opening the eyes of the blind. In such a work, those have light given them who were totally destitute of it before. So in conversion, stones are said to be raised up to children to Abraham; while stones they are altogether destitute of all those qualities that afterwards render them the living children of Abraham, and not only had them not in so great a degree. Agreeably to this, conversion is said to be taking away a heart of stone and giving a heart of flesh. The unconverted man has a heart of stone which has no degree of that life and sense which the heart of flesh has, because it yet remains a stone; nothing is further from life and sense.

INFERENCE 1. From what has been said, I would observe that it must be the case that conversion is wrought at once. The knowledge that reformation and conviction that is preparatory to conversion may be gradual, and the work of grace after conversion may be gradually carried on, yet that work of grace upon the soul whereby a person is brought out of a state of total corruption and depravity into a state of grace, to an interest in Christ, and to be actually a child of God, is in a moment.

It must be the consequence; for if that grace or virtue that a person has when he is brought into a state of grace is entirely different in nature and kind from all that went before, then it will follow that the last instant before a person is actually a child of God and in a state of grace, a person has not the least degree of any real goodness, and of that true virtue that is in a child of God.

Those things by which conversion is represented in Scripture hold forth the same thing. In creation something is brought out of nothing in an instant. God speaks and it is done. He commands and it stands fast. When the dead are raised, it is done in a moment. Thus, when Christ called Lazarus out of his grave, it was not a gradual work. He said, "Lazarus, come forth," and there went life with the call. He heard His voice and lived. So Christ said in John 5:25, "Verily, verily, I say unto you, the hour is coming, and now is, when the dead shall hear the voice of the Son of God; and they that hear shall live," which words must be understood of the work of conversion. In creation, being is called out of nothing and instantly obeys the call, and in the resurrection the dead are called into life. As soon as the call is given the dead obey.

By reason of this instantaneousness of the work of conversion, one of the names under which conversion is frequently spoken of in Scripture is "calling." Romans 8:28–30: "And we know that all things work together for good to them that love God, to them who are

the called according to His purpose. For whom He did
foreknow, He also did predestinate to be conformed to
the image of His Son, that He might be the firstborn
among many brethren. Moreover whom He did predestinate, them He also called; and whom He called, them
He also justified; and whom He justified, them He also
glorified." Acts 2:37–39: "Now when they heard this,
they were pricked in their heart, and said unto Peter,
and to the rest of the apostles, 'Men and brethren, what
shall we do?' Then Peter said into them, 'Repent, and
be baptized every one of you in the name of Jesus Christ
for the remission of sins, and ye shall receive the gift of
the Holy Ghost. For the promise is unto you, and to
your children, and to all that are afar off, even as many
as the Lord our God shall call.' " Hebrews 9:15: "That
they which are called might receive the promise of the
eternal inheritance." 1 Thessalonians 5:23–24: "And the
very God of peace sanctify you wholly . . . faithful is he
that calleth you, who also will do it."

Nothing else can be meant in those places by
"calling" than what Christ does in a sinner's saving
conversion. By this it seems evident that it is done at
once, and not gradually; whereby Christ, through His
great power, does but speak the powerful word and it is
done. He but calls, and the heart of the sinner immediately comes. It seems to be symbolized by Christ's calling His disciples, and their immediately following
Him. So when he called Peter, Andrew, James, and
John, they were minding other things; but at His call
they immediately left all and followed Him (Matthew
4:18–22). Peter and Andrew were casting a net into the
sea, and Christ said to them as He passed by, "Follow
Me." And it is said that they straightway left their nets

and followed Him. So James and John were in the ship with Zebedee their father, mending their nets, and He called them, and immediately they left the ship and their father and followed Him. So it was when Matthew was called. Matthew 9:9: "And as Jesus passed forth from thence, He saw a man named Matthew, sitting at the receipt of custom; and He saith unto him, 'Follow Me.' And he arose and followed Him." Now whether they were then converted or not, yet doubtless Christ, in thus calling His first disciples to a visible following of Him, represents to us the manner in which He would call men to be truly His disciples and spiritually to follow Him in all ages. There is something immediately and instantaneously put into their hearts at that call that they had nothing of before, that effectually disposes them to follow.

It is very manifest that almost all the miracles of Christ that He wrought when on earth were types of His great work of converting sinners, and the manner of His working those miracles holds forth the instantaneousness of the work of conversion. Thus when He healed the leper, which represented His healing us of our spiritual leprosy, He put forth His hand and touched him, and said, "I will; be thou clean." And immediately his leprosy was cleansed (Matthew 8:3; Mark 1:42; Luke 5:13). And so, in opening the eyes of the blind, which represents His opening the eyes of our blind souls (Matthew 20:34), He touched their eyes, and immediately their eyes received sight, and they followed Him (see also Mark 10:52 and Luke 18:43). So when He healed the sick, which represents His healing our spiritual diseases, or conversion, it was done at once. Thus when He healed Simon's wife's mother (Mark 1:31), He took her by the hand and lifted her up; and immediately the fever left her, and she ministered unto them. So when the woman who had the issue of blood touched the hem of Christ's garment, immediately the issue of blood stanched (Luke 8:44). So the woman who was bowed together with the spirit of infirmity, when Christ laid His hands upon her, immediately she was made straight and glorified God (Luke 13:12–13), which represents that action on the soul whereby He gives an upright heart, and sets the soul at liberty from its bondage to glorify Him. So the man at the pool of Bethesda, when Christ bade him rise, take up his bed, and walk, he was immediately made whole (John 5:8–9). After the same manner Christ cast out devils, which represents His dispossessing the devil of our souls in conversion; and so He settled the winds and waves, representing His subduing, in conversion, the heart of the wicked, which is like the troubled sea when it cannot rest. And so He raised the dead, which represented His raising dead souls.

The same is confirmed by those things which conversion is compared to in Scripture. It is often compared to a resurrection. Natural men (as was said before) are said to be dead, and to be raised when they are converted by God's mighty effectual power from the dead. Now, there is no medium point between being dead and alive; he who is dead has no degree of life in him; he who has the least degree of life in him is alive. When a man is raised from the dead, life is not only in a greater degree in him than it was before, but it is all new. The work of conversion seems to be compared to a raising the dead to life in this very thing, even its instantaneousness, or its being done, as it were, at a word being spoken. John 5:25: "Verily, verily, I say unto you, the hour is coming and now is when the dead shall hear the voice of the Son of God, and they that hear shall live." He speaks here of a work of conversion, as appears by the preceding verse, and by the words themselves, which speak of the time of this raising the dead, not only as to come hereafter, but as what was already come. This shows conversion to be an immediate, instantaneous work, like the change made on Lazarus when Christ called him from the grave; there went life with the call, and Lazarus was immediately alive. Immediately before the call, sinners are dead or wholly destitute of life, as appears by the expression, "The dead shall hear the voice," and immediately after the call they are alive. Yea, there goes life with the word, as is evident not only because it is said they shall live, but also because it is said that they shall hear His voice. The first moment they have any life is the moment when Christ calls, and as soon as they are called, which further appears by what was observed before, even that being called and converted are spoken of in Scripture as the same thing.

The same is confirmed from conversion being compared to a work of creation, which is a work wherein something is made either out of nothing, or out of that having no degree of the same kind of qualities and principles, as when God made man of the dust of the earth. Thus it is said, "If any man be in Christ, he is a new creature." This obviously implies that he is an exceedingly different kind of creature from what he was before he was in Christ, that the principle or qualities that he has by which he is a Christian are entirely new, and what there was nothing of before he was in Christ.

INFERENCE 2. Hence we may learn that it is impossible for men to convert themselves by their own strength and industry with only a concurring assistance helping in the exercise of their natural abilities and principles of the soul, and securing their improvement. For what is gained after this manner is a gradual acquisition, and not something instantaneously begotten, and of an entirely different nature, and wholly of a separate kind, from all that was in the nature of the person the moment before. All that men can do by their own strength and industry is only gradually to increase and improve and remodel and direct qualities, principles, and perfections of nature that they have already. And that is evident because a man in the exercise and improvement of the strength and principles of his own nature has nothing but the qualities, powers, and perfections that are already in his nature to work with, and nothing but them to work upon. And therefore it is impossible that by this only anything further should be brought to pass than only a new modification of what is already in the nature of the soul. That which is only by an improvement of natural qualities, principles, and perfections—let those things be improved never so much and never so industriously, and never so long—will still be no more than an improvement of those natural qualities, principles, and perfections; and therefore not anything of an essentially distinct and superior nature and kind.

It is impossible, as Dr. [Samuel] Clarke observes, "that any effect should have any perfection that was not in the cause; for if it had, then that perfection would be caused by nothing."* It is therefore utterly impossible that men's natural perfections and qualities in that exercise, and however assisted in that exercise, should produce in the soul a principle or perfection of a nature entirely different from all of them, or any manner of improvement or modification of them.

The qualities and principles of natural bodies, such as figure or motion, can never produce anything beyond themselves. If infinite comprehensions and divisions are eternally made, the things must still be eternally the same, and all their possible effects can never be anything but repetitions of the same. Nothing can be produced by only those qualities of figure and motion, beyond figure and motion; and so nothing can be produced in the soul by only its internal principles beyond these principles or qualities, or new improvements and modifications of them.

And if we suppose a concurring assistance to enable to a more full and perfect exercise of those natural principles and qualities, unless the assistance or influence actually produces something beyond the exercise of internal principle, still it is the same thing. Nothing will be produced but an improvement and new modification of those principles that are exercised. Therefore it follows that saving grace in the heart can't be produced in man by mere exercise of what perfections he has in him already, though never so much assisted by moral persuasion, and never so much assisted in the exercise of his natural principles, unless there is some-

---

* The well-known *a priori* argument of this eminent thinker (if somewhat uncertain divine), is found in *A Demonstration of the Being and Attributes of God.*

thing more than all this, an immediate infusion or operation of the divine Being upon the soul. Grace must
be the immediate work of God, and properly a produc-
tion of His almighty power on the soul.

Chapter 2

Wherein all saving grace summarily consists

The next thing that arises for consideration is, what is the nature of this Divine principle in the soul that is so entirely diverse from all that is naturally in the soul?

1. The saving grace that is in the hearts of the saints, that within them which is above nature, and entirely distinguishes them from all unconverted men, is radically but one—i.e., however various its exercises are, yet it is but one in its root; it is one individual principle in the heart.

It is common for us to speak of various graces of the Spirit of God as though they were so many different principles of holiness, and to call them by such distinct names as repentance, humility, resignation, thankfulness, and so forth. But we err if we imagine that these, in their first source and root in the heart, are properly distinct principles. They all come from the same fountain and are, indeed, the various exertions and conditions of the same thing, only different denominations according to the various occasions, objects, and manners, attendants and circumstances of its exercise. There is one holy principle in the heart that is the essence and sum of all grace, the root and source of all holy acts of every kind, and the fountain of every good stream into which all Christian virtues may ultimately be resolved, and in which all duty and all holiness is fulfilled.

Thus the Scripture represents it. Grace in the soul is one fountain of the water of life (John 4:14), and not various distinct fountains. So God, in the work of regeneration, implants one heavenly seed in the soul, and not various different seeds. 1 John 3:9: "Whosoever is born of God doth not commit sin; for His seed remaineth in him." The day that has arisen on the soul is but one. The oil in the vessel is simple and pure, conferred by one holy anointing. All is wrought by one individual work of the Spirit of God. And thus it is there is an agreement of graces. Not only is one grace in some way allied to another, and so tends to help and promote one another, but one is really implied in the other. The nature of one involves the nature of another. And the great reason of it is that all graces have one common essence, the original principle of all, and is but one. Strip the various parts of the Christian soul of their circumstances, concomitants, appendages, means, and occasions, and consider that which is, as it were, their soul and essence, and all appears to be the same.

2. That principle which is in the soul of the saints, which is the grand Christian virtue, and which is the soul and essence and summary comprehension of all grace, is a principle of divine love. This is evident because we are abundantly taught in the Scripture that divine love is the sum of all duty; and that all that God requires of us is fulfilled in it. Love is the sum of all the duty of the heart, and its exercises and fruits the sum of all the duty of life. But if the duty of the heart, or all due dispositions of hearts, are all summed up in love, then undoubtedly all grace may be summed up in love.

The Scripture teaches us that all our duty is summed up in love, or, which is the same thing, that it is the sum of all that is required in the Law; and that is true whether we take the Law as signifying the Ten Commandments or the whole written Word of God. So it is when by the Law is meant the Ten Commandments. Romans 13:8: "Owe no man anything, but to love one another; for he that loveth another hath fulfilled the Law"; and, therefore, several of these commandments are there rehearsed. And again in verse 10: "Love is the fulfilling of the Law." And unless love was the sum of what the Law required, the Law could not be fulfilled in love. A law is not fulfilled but by obedience to the sum of what it contains. So the same apostle writes again in 1 Timothy 1:5: "Now the end of the commandment is charity [love]."

If we take the Law in a yet more extensive sense for the whole written Word of God, the Scripture still teaches us that love is the sum of what is required in it. Thus in Matthew 22:40 Christ teaches us that on the two precepts of loving God and our neighbor hang all the Law and the Prophets, that is, all the written Word of God. So that what was called "the Law and the Prophets" was the whole written Word of God that was then extant. The Scripture teaches this of each table of the Law in particular.

Thus the lawyer that we read of in Luke 10:25–28 mentions the love of God and our neighbor as the sum of the two tables of the Law; and Christ approves of what he says. When he stood up and tempted Christ with the question, "Master, what shall I do to inherit eternal life?" Christ asked him what was required of him "in the Law?" He answered, "Thou shalt love the Lord thy God with all thy heart, and with all thy soul, and with all thy strength, and with all thy mind, and thy neighbor as thyself." And Christ replied, "Thou hast answered right; this do, and thou shalt live." This was as much as if He had said, "Do this, and then thou hast fulfilled the whole Law."

So in Matthew 22:36–38, that commandment, "Thou shalt love the Lord thy God with all thy heart, and with all thy soul, and with all thy mind," is given by Christ Himself as the sum of the first table of the Law in answer to the question of the lawyer who asked Him, "Which is the great commandment of the Law?" And in the next verse, loving our neighbors as ourselves is mentioned as the sum of the second table, as it is also in Romans 13:9, where most of the precepts of the second table are rehearsed over in particular: "Thou shalt not commit adultery. Thou shalt not kill. Thou shalt not steal. Thou shalt not bear false witness. Thou shalt not covet. And if there is any other commandment, it is briefly comprehended in this saying, namely, 'Thou shalt love thy neighbor as thyself.' "

The Apostle James seems to teach the same thing. James 2:8: "If ye fulfill the royal law according to the Scripture, 'Thou shalt love thy neighbor as thyself,' ye do well."

Thus frequent, express, and particular is the Scripture in teaching us that all duty is comprehended in love. The Scripture teaches us in like manner of nothing else. This is quite another thing than if religion in general had only sometimes gone under the name of "the love of God," as it sometimes goes by the name of "the fear of God," sometimes "the knowledge of God," and sometimes "feeling of God."

This argument fully and irrefragably proves that all grace, and every Christian disposition and habit of mind and heart, especially as to that which is primarily holy and divine in it, summarily consists in divine love, and may be resolved into it; however, with respect to its kinds and manner of exercise and its appendages, it may be diversified. For certainly there is no duty of heart, or due disposition of mind, but what is included in the "Law and the Prophets," and is required by some precept of that law and rule which He has given mankind to walk by. But yet the Scripture affords us other evidences of the truth of this.

The apostle speaks of divine love as that which is the essence of all Christianity in 1 Corinthians 13. The apostle evidently means a comparison between the gifts of the Spirit and the grace of the Spirit. In the foregoing chapter the apostle had been speaking of the gifts of the Spirit throughout—such as the gift of wisdom, the gift of knowledge, the gift of faith, the gift of healing or working miracles, prophecy, discerning spirits, speaking with tongues, and so forth—and in the last verse in the chapter he exhorts the Corinthians to "covet earnestly the best gifts," but adds, "and yet I show you a more excellent way," and so proceeds to discourse of the saving grace of the Spirit under the name of "agape" (love), and to compare this saving grace in the heart with those gifts. Now it is manifest that the comparison is between the gifts of the Spirit that were common to both saints and sinners and that saving grace that distinguishes true saints; and therefore charity (or love) is here understood by divines as intending the same thing as sincere grace of heart.

By love or charity here there is no reason to understand the apostle as speaking only of love to men, but that principle of divine love that is in the heart of the saints in the full extent, which primarily has God for its object. For there is no reason to think that the apostle doesn't mean the same thing by charity here as he does in the 8th chapter of the same epistle, where he is comparing the same two things together, knowledge and charity, as he does here. But there he explains himself to mean by charity the love of God (verses 1–3): "Now, as touching things offered unto idols, we know that we all have knowledge. Knowledge puffeth up, but charity edifieth. And if any man think that he knoweth anything, he knoweth nothing yet as he ought to know. But if any man love God, the same is known of Him."

It is manifest that love (or charity) is in chapter 13 spoken of as the very essence of all Christianity, and is the very thing wherein a gracious sincerity consists. For the apostle speaks of it as the most excellent, the most necessary and essential thing of all, without which all that makes the greatest, fairest, and most glittering show in religion is nothing—without which, if we speak with the tongues of men and angels, we have become as sounding brass and tinkling cymbals, and without which, though we have the gift of prophecy, and understand all mysteries and all knowledge, and have all faith, so that we could remove mountains, and should bestow all our goods to feed the poor, and even give our bodies to be burned, we are nothing. Therefore, how can we understand the apostle in any other way than that this is the very thing whereof the essence of all consists, and that he means the same by charity as a gracious charity, as indeed it is generally understood. If a man does all these things here spoken of—makes such glorious prophecies, has such knowledge, such faith, speaks so excellently, performs such excellent external acts, and does such great things in religion as giving all his goods to the poor and giving his body to be burned—what is wanting but one thing? The very quintessence of all religion, the very thing wherein lies summarily the sincerity, spirituality, and divinity of religion, and that, the apostle teaches us, is love.

And further, it is manifestly the apostle's drift to show how this excellent principle radically comprehends all that is good. For he goes on to show how all essences of good and excellent dispositions and exercises, both towards God and towards man, are virtually contained and will flow from this one principle: "Love suffereth long, and is kind, envieth not . . . endureth all things." The words of this last verse especially respect duties to God, as the former did duties to men, as I would show more particularly afterwards.

Here it may be noted, by the way, that by charity "believing all things, hoping all things," the apostle has, undoubtedly, respect to the same faith and hope that in other parts of the chapter are mentioned together and compared with charity (as I think might sufficiently be made manifest if it were here proper to spend time on it). And not believing and hoping, in the case of our neighbor, which the apostle had spoken of before, in the last words of verse 5, and had plainly summed up all parts of charity towards our neighbor in verse 6. And then, in this verse, the apostle proceeds to mention other exercises or fruits of charity that are of quite another kind: patience under suffering, faith, hope, and perseverance.

Thus the apostle doesn't only represent love or charity as the most excellent thing in Christianity, and as the quintessence, life, and soul of all religion, but as

that which virtually comprehends all holy virtues and
exercises. And because love is the quintessence and
soul of all grace, wherein the divinity and holiness of
all that belongs to charity properly and essentially consists, therefore, when Christians come to be in their
most perfect state, and the divine nature in them shall
be in its greatest exaltation and purity, and be free from
all mixtures, stripped of these appurtenances and that
clothing that it has in the present state; and when it
shall lose many other of its denominations, especially
from the peculiar manner and exercises accommo-
dated to the imperfect circumstances of the present
state, they will be what will remain. All other names will
be swallowed up in the name of charity or love, as the
apostle, agreeably to his chapter on this (1 Corinthians
13) observes in verses 8–10: "Charity never faileth. But
when that which is perfect is come, then that which is
in part shall be done away." And, therefore, when the
apostle, in the last verse, speaks of charity as the greatest grace, we may well understand him in the same
sense as when Christ speaks of the command to love
God as being the greatest commandment, that is, that
among the graces, that is the source and sum of all
graces, as that commanded is spoken of as the sum of
all commands, and requiring that duty which is the
ground of all other duties.

It must be because charity is the quintessence and
soul of all duty and all good in the heart that the apostle says that it is "the end of the commandment," for
doubtless the main end of the commandment is to
promote that which is most essential in religion and
constituent of holiness.

3. Reason bears witness to the same thing. Reason

testifies that divine love is so essential in religion that all religion is but hypocrisy and a "vain show" without it. What is religion but the exercise and expressions of regard to the divine Being? But certainly if there is no love to Him, there is no sincere regard to Him; and all pretenses and show of respect to Him, whether it be in word or deed, must be hypocrisy, and of no value in the eyes of Him who sees the heart. How manifest is it that without love there can be no true honor, no sincere praise! And how can obedience be hearty if it is not a testimony of respect to God? The fear of God without love is nothing other than the fear of devils; and all that outward respect and obedience, all that resignation, that repentance and sorrow for sin, that form in religion, that outward devotion that is performed merely from such a fear without love, is all of it a practical lie. Psalm 66:3: "How terrible art Thou in Thy works! Through the greatness of Thy power shall Thine enemies submit themselves unto Thee." In the original it is "shall Thine enemies lie unto Thee," i.e., "shall yield a feigned or lying obedience and respect to Thee," while still they remain enemies in their hearts. There is never a devil in hell but who would perform all that many a man has performed in religion who had no love to God—and a great deal more if they were in like circumstances and the like hope of gain by it, and be as much of a devil in his heart as he is now. The devil in Luke 8:28 seemed to be religious from fear of torment: "When he saw Jesus, he cried out, and fell down before Him, and with a loud voice said, 'What have I to do with Thee, Jesus, Thou Son of God Most High? I beseech Thee, torment me not.' " Here is external worship. The devil is religious; he prays, and he prays in a humble posture; he falls down before Christ; he lies prostrate; he prays earnestly, he cries with a loud voice; he uses humble expressions: "I beseech Thee, torment me not." He uses respectful, honorable, adoring expressions: "Jesus, Thou Son of God Most High." Nothing was wanting but love.

And with respect to duties towards men, no good offices would be accepted by men one from another if they saw the heart, and knew they did not proceed from any respect in the heart. If a child carries it very respectfully to his father, either from a strong fear or from hope of having the larger inheritance when his father is dead, or from a like consideration, and not at all from any respect to his father in his heart; if the child's heart were open to the view of his father, and he plainly knew that there was no real regard to him, would the child's outward honor and obedience be acceptable to the parent? So if a wife should carry it very well to her husband, and not at all from any love to him, but from other considerations plainly seen, and certainly known by the husband, would he at all delight in her outward respect any more than if a wooden image were contrived to make respectful motions in his presence?

If duties towards men are to be accepted by God as a part of religion and the service of the divine Being, they must be performed not only with a hearty love to men, but that love must flow from regard to Him.

Reason shows that all good dispositions and duties are wholly comprehended in, and will flow from, divine love. Love to God and men implies all proper respect or regard to God and men; and all proper acts and expressions of regard to both will flow from it, and therefore all duty to both. To regard God and men in our heart as we ought, and to have that nature of heart towards them that we ought, is the same thing. And therefore, a proper regard or love comprehends all virtue of heart; and he who shows all proper regard to God and men in his practice performs all that in practice towards them which is his duty. The apostle says in Romans 13:10, "Love works no ill to his neighbor." It is evident by his reasoning in that place that he means more than is expressed—that love works no ill, but all good, all our duty to our neighbor, which reason plainly shows. And as the apostle teaches that love to our neighbor works no ill, but all good towards our neighbor, so, by a parity of reason, love to God works no ill, but all our duty towards God.

A Christian love to God and Christian love to men are not properly two distinct principles in the heart. These varieties are radically the same: the same principle flowing forth towards different objects, according to the order of their existence. God is the First Cause of all things, and the Fountain and Source of all good; and men are derived from Him, having something of His image, and are the objects of His mercy. So the first and supreme object of divine Love is God; and men are loved either as the children of God or as His creatures, those who are in His image, the objects of His mercy, in some respects related to God, partakers of His loveliness, or at least capable of happiness.

That love to God and a Christian love to men are thus but one in their root and foundation-principle in the heart is confirmed by several passages in 1 John 3:16–17: "Hereby perceive we the love of God, because He laid down His life for us; and we ought to lay down our lives for the brethren. But whoso hath this world's

goods . . . how dwelleth the love of God in him?"
Chapter 4:20–21: "If a man say, 'I love God,' and hateth
his brother, he is a liar; for he that loveth not his
brother whom he hath seen, how can he love God
whom he hath not seen? And this commandment have
we from Him, that he who loveth God love his brother
also." Chapter 5:1–2: "Whosoever believeth that Jesus is
the Christ is born of God; and every one that loveth
Him that begat loveth him also that is begotten of Him.
By this we know that we love the children of God, when
we love God, and keep His commandments."

Therefore, to explain the nature of divine love, what
is principally requisite is to explain the nature of love
to God. For this may especially be called divine love;
and herein all Christian love or charity radically consists, for this is the fountain of all.

As for a definition of divine love, things of this nature are not properly capable of a definition. They are
better felt than defined. Love is a term as clear in its
significance, and that as naturally suggests to the mind
the thing signified by it, as any other term or terms that
we can find out or substitute in its place. Yet there may
be a great deal of benefit in descriptions that may be
given of this heavenly principle, though they all are
imperfect. They may serve to limit the significance of
the term, to distinguish this principle from other
things, to exclude counterfeits, and also more clearly to
explain some things that pertain to its nature.

Divine love, as it has God for its object, may be thus
described: it is the soul's relish of the supreme excellency of the divine nature, inclining the heart to God
as the chief good.

The first thing in divine love, and that from which

everything which pertains to it arises, is a relish of the excellency of the divine nature, which the soul of man by nature has nothing of.

The first effect that is produced in the soul, whereby it is carried above what it has or can have by nature, is to cause it to relish or taste the sweetness of the divine relation. That is the first and most fundamental thing in divine love, and that from which everything else that belongs to divine love naturally and necessarily proceeds. Once the soul is brought to relish the excellency of the divine nature, then it will naturally, and of course, incline to God in every way. It will incline to be with Him and to enjoy Him. It will have benevolence to God. It will be glad that He is happy. It will incline that He should be glorified, and that His will should be done in all things. So that the first effect of the power of God in the heart in regeneration is to give the heart a divine taste or sense, to cause it to have a relish of the loveliness and sweetness of the supreme excellency of the divine nature; and indeed this is all the immediate effect of the divine power that there is; this is all the Spirit of God needs to do in order to produce all good effects in the soul. If God, by an immediate act of His, gives the soul a relish of the excellency of His own nature, other things will follow of themselves without any further act of the divine power than only what is necessary to uphold the nature of the faculties of the soul. He who has once been brought to see, or rather to taste, the superlative loveliness of the Divine Being, will need no more to make him long after the enjoyment of God, to make him rejoice in the happiness of God, and to desire that this supremely excellent Being may be pleased and glorified.

Love is commonly distinguished into a love of complacence and a love of benevolence. Of these two a love of complacence is first, and is the foundation of the other, if by a love of complacence is meant relishing a sweetness in the qualifications of the beloved, and being pleased and delighted in his excellency. This, in the order of nature, is before benevolence, because it is the foundation and reason of it. A person must first relish that wherein the amiableness of nature consists before he can wish well to him on account of that loveliness, or as being worthy to receive good. Indeed, sometimes love of complacence is explained as something differently, even for that joy that the soul has in the presence and possession of the beloved, which is different from the soul's relish of the beauty of the beloved, and is a fruit of it, as benevolence is. The soul may relish the sweetness and the beauty of a beloved object whether that object is present or absent, whether in possession or not in possession; and this relish is the foundation of love of benevolence, or desire of the good of the beloved. It is the foundation of love or affection to the beloved object when absent; it is the foundation of one's rejoicing in the object when present; and so it is the foundation of everything else that belongs to divine love.

And if this is true, then the main ground of true love to God is the excellency of His own nature, and not any benefit we have received or hope to receive by His goodness to us. Not but that there is such a thing as a gracious gratitude to God for mercies bestowed upon us; and the acts and fruits of His goodness to us may be, and very often are, occasions and incitements of the exercise of true love to God, as I must show more particularly hereafter. But love or affection to God that has no other good than only some benefit received or hoped for from God is not true love. If it is without any sense of a delight in the absolute excellency of the divine nature, it has nothing divine in it. Such gratitude towards God requires no more to be in the soul than that human nature that all men are born with, or at least that human nature well cultivated and improved, or indeed not further vitiated and depraved than it naturally is.

It is possible that natural men, without the addition of any further principle than they have by nature, may be affected with gratitude by some remarkable kindness of God to them, as that they should be so affected with some great act of kindness of a neighbor. A principle of self-love is all that is necessary to both. But divine love is a principle distinct from self-love, and from all that arises from it. Indeed, after a man has come to relish the sweetness of the supreme good there is in the nature of God, self-love may have a hand in an appetite after the enjoyment of that good. For self-love will necessarily make a man desire to enjoy that which is sweet to him. But God's perfections must first savor the appetite and be sweet to men, or they must first have a taste to relish sweetness in the perfection of God, before self-love can have any influence upon them to cause an appetite after the enjoyment of that sweetness. And, therefore, that divine taste or relish of the soul wherein divine love most fundamentally consists is prior to all influence that self-love can have to incline us to God, and so must be a principle quite distinct from it and independent of it.

Chapter 3

How a principle of grace is from the Spirit of God

That this holy and divine principle, which we have shown radically and summarily consists in divine love, comes into existence in the soul by the power of God in the influences of the Holy Spirit, the Third Person in the blessed Trinity, is abundantly manifest from the Scriptures.

Regeneration is by the Spirit. John 3:5–6: "Verily, verily, I say unto thee, except a man be born of water, and of the Spirit, he cannot enter into the kingdom of God. That which is born of the flesh is flesh; and that which is born of the Spirit is spirit." And verse 8: "The wind bloweth where it listeth, and thou hearest the sound thereof, but canst not tell whence it cometh, and whither it goest; so is every one that is born of the Spirit."

The renewing of the soul is by the Holy Ghost. Titus 3:5: "Not by works of righteousness which we have done, but according to His mercy He saved us, by the washing of regeneration, and renewing of the Holy Ghost."

A new heart is given by God's putting His Spirit within us. Ezekiel 36:26–27: "A new heart also will I give you, and a new spirit will I put within you; and I will take away the stony heart out of your flesh, and I will give you a heart of flesh. And I will put my Spirit within you, and cause you to walk in my statutes, and ye shall keep My judgments and do them."

Quickening of the dead soul is by the Spirit. John 6:63: "It is the Spirit that quickeneth."

Sanctification is by the Spirit of God. 2 Thessalonians 2:13: "God hath from the beginning chosen you to salvation through sanctification of the Spirit, and belief of the truth." Romans 15:16: "That the offering up of the Gentiles might be acceptable, being sanctified by the Holy Ghost." 1 Corinthians 6:11: "Such were some of you, but ye are washed, but ye are sanctified, but ye are justified in the name of the Lord Jesus, and by the Spirit of our God." 1 Peter 1:2: "Elect according to the foreknowledge of God the Father, through sanctification of the Spirit, unto obedience and sprinkling of the blood of Jesus Christ."

All grace in the heart is the fruit of the Spirit. Galatians 5:22–23: "But the fruit of the Spirit is love, joy, peace, long-suffering, gentleness, goodness, faith, meekness, temperance." Ephesians 5:9: "The fruit of the Spirit is in all goodness, and righteousness, and truth." Hence the Spirit of God is called the Spirit of grace in Hebrews 10:29.

This doctrine of a gracious nature being by the immediate influence of the Spirit of God is not only taught in the Scriptures, but is undeniable to reason. Indeed there seems to be a strong disposition in men to disbelieve and oppose the doctrine of true disposition, to disbelieve and oppose the doctrine of immediate influence of the Spirit of God in the hearts of men, or to diminish and make it as small and remote a matter as possible, and put it as far out of sight as may be. Whereas, it seems to me, true virtue and holiness would naturally excite a prejudice (if I may so say) in favor of such a doctrine; and that the soul, when in the most excellent frame, and the most lively exercise of virtue— love to God and delight in Him—would naturally and unavoidably think of God as kindly communicating Himself to him, and holding communion with him, as though he did as it were see God smiling on him, giving to him and conversing with him; and that if he did not so think of God, but, on the contrary, should conceive that there was no immediate communication between God and him, it would tend greatly to quell his holy motions of soul, and be an exceeding damage to his pleasure.

No good reason can be given why men should have such an inward disposition to deny any immediate communication between God and the creature, or to make as little of it as possible. It is a strange disposition that men have to thrust God out of the world, or to put Him as far out of sight as they can, and to have in no respect immediately and sensibly to do with Him. Therefore so many schemes have been drawn to exclude, extenuate, or remove at a great distance any influence of the Divine Being in the hearts of men, such as the scheme of the Pelagians, the Socinians, and others. And therefore doctrines are so ridiculed that ascribe much to the immediate influence of the Spirit, those called "enthusiasm," "fanaticism," "whimsy," and "distraction"; but no mortal can tell for what.

If we make no difficulty of allowing that God immediately made the whole universe at first, and caused it to exist out of nothing, and that every individual thing owes its being to an immediate, voluntary, arbitrary act of Almighty power, why should we make a difficulty of supposing that He has still something immediately to do with the things that He has made, and that there is an arbitrary influence still that God has in the creation that He has made?

And if it is reasonable to suppose it with respect to any part of the creation, it is especially so with respect to reasonable creatures, who are the highest part of the creation, next to God, who are most immediately made for God, who have Him for their next Head, and are created for the business wherein they are mostly concerned. And above all, this is so in that wherein the highest excellency of this highest rank of beings consists, and that wherein he is most conformed to God is nearest to Him and has God for his most immediate object.

It seems to me most rational to suppose that as we ascend in the order of being we shall at last come immediately to God, the First Cause. In whatever respect we ascend, we ascend in the order of time and succession.

The Scripture speaks of this holy and divine principle in the heart as not only from the Spirit, but as being spiritual. Thus saving knowledge is called spiritual understanding. Colossians 1:9: "We desire that ye might be filled with the knowledge of His will in all wisdom and spiritual understanding." So the influences, graces, and comforts of God's Spirit are called spiritual blessings. Ephesians 1:3: "Blessed be the God and Father of our Lord Jesus Christ, who hath blessed us with all spiritual blessings in heavenly places in Christ." So the imparting of any gracious benefit is called the imparting of a spiritual gift. Romans 1:11: "For I long to see you, that I may impart unto you some spiritual gift." The fruits of the Spirit which are offered to God are called

spiritual sacrifices. 1 Peter 2:5: "A spiritual priesthood
to offer up spiritual sacrifices, acceptable to God by
Jesus Christ." A spiritual person signifies the same in
Scripture as a gracious person, and sometimes one who
is much under the influence of grace. 1 Corinthians
2:15: "He that is spiritual judgeth all things, yet he himself is judged of no man." And 3:1: "And I, brethren,
could not speak unto you as unto spiritual but as unto
carnal." Galatians 6:1: "If a man be overtaken in a fault,
ye which are spiritual restore such an one in the spirit
of meekness." And to be graciously minded is called in
Scripture being spiritually minded. Romans 8:6: "To be
spiritual minded is life and peace."

Concerning this, two things are to be noted:

1. This divine principle in the heart is not called
spiritual because it has its seat in the soul or spiritual
part of man, and not in his body. It is called spiritual,
not because of its relation to the spirit of man in which
it is, but because of its relation to the Spirit of God from
which it is. That things are not called spiritual because
they pertain not to the body but the spirit of man is evident, because gracious or holy understanding is called
spiritual understanding in the forementioned passage
(Colossians 1:9). Now, by spiritual understanding cannot be meant that understanding which has its seat in
the soul, to distinguish it from other understanding
that has its seat in the body; for all understanding has
its seat in the soul; and that things are called spiritual
because of their relation to the Spirit of God is most
plain by the latter part of 1 Corinthians 2. There we
have both those expressions, one immediately after another, evidently meaning the same thing. Verses 13–14:
"Which things also we speak, not in the words which

man's wisdom teacheth, but which the Holy Ghost teacheth; comparing spiritual things with spiritual. But
the natural man receiveth not the things of the Spirit
of God." And that by the spiritual man is meant one
who has the Spirit is also as plainly evident by the context. Verses 10–12: "God hath revealed them unto us by
His Spirit; for the Spirit searcheth all things, yea, the
deep things of God. For what man knoweth the things
of a man . . . ?" Also verse 15: "He that is spiritual judgeth all things," by which is evidently meant the same
as "he that hath the Spirit that searcheth all things," as
we find in the foregoing verses. So persons are said to
be spiritually-minded not because they mind things
that relate to the soul or spirit of man, but because they
mind things that relate to the Spirit of God. Romans
8:5–6: "For they that are after the flesh do mind the
things of the flesh; but they that are after the Spirit the
things of the Spirit. For to be carnally minded is death;
but to be spiritually minded is life and peace."

2. It must be observed that, where this holy, divine
principle of saving grace wrought in the mind is in
Scripture called spiritual, what is intended by the expression is not merely nor chiefly that it is from the
Spirit of God, but that it is of the nature of the Spirit of
God. There are many things in the minds of some natural men that are from the influence of the Spirit, but
yet are by no means spiritual things in the scriptural
sense of the word. The Spirit of God convinces natural
men of sin (John 16:8). Natural men may have common
grace, common illuminations, and common affections
that are from the Spirit of God, as appears from
Hebrews 6:4. Natural men have sometimes the influences of the Spirit of God in His common operations

and gifts, and therefore God's Spirit is said to be striv-
ing with them, and they are said to resist the Spirit
(Acts 7:51); to grieve and vex God's Holy Spirit
(Ephesians 4:30; Isaiah 63:10); and God is said to depart
from them even as the Spirit of the Lord departed from
Saul. 1 Samuel 16:14: "But the Spirit of the Lord departed from Saul, and an evil spirit from the Lord troubled him."

But yet natural men are not in any degree spiritual.
The great difference between natural men and godly
men seems to be set forth by this: that the one is natural and carnal, and the other spiritual. Natural men are
so totally destitute of that which is Spirit that they know
nothing about it, and the reason given for it is because
they are not spiritual (1 Corinthians 2:13–15). Indeed,
sometimes those miraculous gifts of the Spirit that were
common are called spiritual because they are from the
Spirit of God. But for the most part the term seems to
be appropriated to its gracious influences and fruits on
the soul, which are no otherwise spiritual than the
common influences of the Spirit that natural men
have, in any other respect than this, that this saving
grace in the soul is not only from the Spirit, but it also
partakes of the nature of that Spirit that it is from,
which the common grace of the Spirit does not. Thus
things in Scripture language are said to be earthly as
they partake of an earthly nature, partake of the nature
of the earth; so things are said to be heavenly as they, in
their nature, agree with those things that are in
heaven. So saving grace in the heart is said to be spiritual, and therein distinguished from all other influences of the Spirit, that it is of the nature of the Spirit
of God. It partakes of the nature of that Spirit while no

common gift of the Spirit does so.

QUESTION. How does saving grace partake of the nature of that Spirit that it is from, so as to be called on that account spiritual, thus essentially distinguishing it from all other effects of the Spirit? For every effect has in some respect or another the nature of its cause, and the common convictions and illuminations that natural men have are in some respects of the nature of the Spirit of God; for there is light and understanding and conviction of truth in these common illuminations, and so they are of the nature of the spirit of God, that is, a discerning spirit and a spirit of truth. But yet saving grace, by its being called spiritual, as though it were thereby distinguished from all other gifts of the Spirit, seems to partake of the nature of the Spirit of God in some very peculiar manner.

ANSWER. To clearly satisfy this inquiry, we must do these two things:

First, we must bear in mind what has already been said of the nature of saving grace, and what I have already shown to be that wherein its nature and essence lies, and wherein all saving grace is radically and summarily comprised—a principle of divine love.

Second, we must consider what the Scripture reveals to be, in a peculiar manner, the nature of the Holy Spirit of God. And in an inquiry of this nature I would go no further than I think the Scripture plainly goes before me. The Word of God certainly should be our rule in matters so much above reason and our own notions.

And here I would say that I think the Scripture sufficiently reveals the Holy Spirit as a proper divine Person; and thus we ought to look upon Him as a distinct, per-

sonal agent. He is often spoken of as a person, revealed
under personal characteristics and in personal acts,
and it speaks of His being acted on as a person. The
Scripture plainly ascribes everything to Him that properly denotes a distinct person; and though the word
"person" is rarely used in the Scriptures, yet I believe
that we have no word in the English language that so
naturally represents what the Scripture reveals of the
distinction of the Eternal Three (Father, Son, and Holy
Ghost) as to say they are one God, but three persons.

Though all the divine perfections are to be at-
tributed to each person of the Trinity, yet the Holy
Ghost is in a peculiar manner called by the name of
"love" (agape), the same word that is translated
"charity" in 1 Corinthians 13. The Godhead, or the divine essence, is once and again said to be love. 1 John
4:8: "He that loveth not knoweth not God; for God is
love." So again in verse 16: "God is love; and he that
dwelleth in love, dwelleth in God, and God in him." But
the divine essence is thus called in a peculiar manner
as breathed forth and subsisting in the Holy Spirit, as
may be seen in the context of these texts, as in verses
12–13 of that same chapter: "No man hath seen God at
any time. If we love one another, God dwelleth in us,
and His love is perfected in us. Hereby know we that we
dwell in Him, and He in us, because He hath given us
of His Spirit." It is the same argument in both these
verses: in verse 12 the apostle argues that if we have love
dwelling in us, we have God dwelling in us; in verse 13
he clears the face of the argument by this, that this love
which is dwelling in us is God's Spirit. And this shows
that the foregoing argument is good, and that if love
dwells in us, you know God dwells in us indeed; for the

apostle supposes it as something granted and allowed that God's Spirit is God. The Scripture elsewhere abundantly teaches us that the way in which God dwells in the saints is by His Spirit, by their being the temples of the Holy Ghost. Here this apostle teaches us the same thing. He says, "We know that He dwelleth in us, that He hath given us His Spirit"; and this is manifestly to explain what is said in the foregoing verse, that God dwells in us inasmuch as His love dwells in us. This love, he had told us before in verse 8, is God Himself. And afterwards, in verse 16, he expresses more fully that this is the way that God dwells in the saint, because this love dwells in them, which is God.

Again, the same is signified in the same manner in the last verses of the foregoing chapter. In the foregoing verses, speaking of love as a true sign of sincerity and our acceptance with God, beginning with verse 13, he sums up the argument thus: "And hereby we know that He abideth in us, by the Spirit which He hath given us."

We have also something very much like this in the Apostle Paul's writings. Galatians 5:13–16: "Use not liberty for an occasion to the flesh, but by love serve one another. For all the law is fulfilled in one word, even in this, thou shalt love thy neighbor as thyself. But if ye bite and devour one another, take heed that ye be not consumed one of another. This I say then, walk in the Spirit, and ye shall not fulfill the lust of the flesh." Here it seems most evident that what the apostle exhorts and urges in verses 13–15, that they should walk in love so that they might not give occasion to the gratifying of the flesh, he expressly explains in the verse 16 by this, that they should walk in the Spirit that they might not

fulfill the lust of the flesh. The great Mr. [John] Howe
takes notice of this in his *Sermons on the Prosperous State of
the Christian Interest Before the End of Time.** His words are,
"Walking in the Spirit is directed with a special eye and
reference unto the exercise of this love; as you may see
in Galatians 5, the 14th, 15th and 16th verses compared
together. All the law is fulfilled in one word (he means
the whole law of the second table), even in this, 'Thou
shalt love thy neighbor as thyself.' But if ye bite and devour one another (the opposite to this love, or that
which follows on the want of it, or from the opposite
principle), take heed that ye be not consumed one of
another. This I say then (observe the inference), Walk
in the Spirit, and ye shall not fulfill the lust of the flesh.
To walk in the Spirit is to walk in the exercise of this
love."

As the Son of God is spoken of as the wisdom, understanding and Logos of God (Proverbs 8; Luke 11:49;
John 1:1-4) and is, as divines express things, the personal Wisdom of God, so the Spirit of God is spoken of
as the Love of God, and may with equal foundation and
propriety be called the personal Love of God. We read
in the beloved disciple's writings of these two, *logos* and
agape, both of which are said to be God (John 1:1; 1
John 4:8–16). One is the Son of God, and the other the
Holy Spirit. There are two things that God is said to be
in 1 John: light and love. Chapter 1:5: "God is light."
This is the Son of God, who is said to be the wisdom
and reason of God, and the brightness of His glory; and
in the 4th chapter of the same epistle he says, "God is

---

* This work is not in the standard 3 volume edition of Howe's
Works, but is part of what is known as Howe's *Posthumous Works.*

love," and this he applies to the Holy Spirit.

Hence the Scripture symbol of the Holy Ghost is a dove, which is the emblem of love, and so was continually accounted (as is well known) in the heathen world, and is so made use of by their poets and mythologists, which probably arose partly from the nature and manner of the bird, and probably in part from the tradition of the story of Noah's dove, that came with a message of peace and love after such terrible manifestations of God's wrath in the time of the deluge. This bird is also made use of as an emblem of love in the Holy Scriptures, as it was on that message of peace and love that God sent it to Noah, when it came with an olive leaf in its mouth, and often in Solomon's Song. Song of Solomon 1:15: "Thou hast doves' eyes." Song of Solomon 5:12: "His eyes are as the eyes of doves." Song of Solomon 5:2: "Open to me, my love, my dove," and in other places in that song.

This bird God is pleased to choose as the special symbol of His Holy Spirit in the greatest office or work of the Spirit that ever it has or will exert—in anointing Christ, the great Head of the whole Church of saints, from which Head this holy oil descends to all the members, and the skirts of His garments, as the sweet and precious ointment that was poured on Aaron's head, that great type of Christ. As God the Father then poured forth His Holy Spirit of love upon the Son without measure, so that which was then seen with the eye—a dove descending and lighting upon Christ— signified the same thing as what was at the same time proclaimed to the Son, "This is my beloved Son, in whom I am well pleased"—"This is the Son on whom I pour forth all My love, towards whom My essence en-

tirely flows out in love" (see Matthew 3:16–17; Mark 1:
10–11; Luke 3:22; John 1:32–33).

This was the anointing of the Head of the Church
and our great High Priest, and therefore the holy
anointing oil of old with which Aaron and other typi-
cal high priests were anointed was the most eminent
type of the Holy Spirit of any in the Old Testament.
This holy oil, by reason of its soft-flowing and diffusive
nature, and its unparalleled sweetness and fragrance,
most fitly represented divine love, or that Spirit that is
the Deity, breathed forth or flowing out and softly
falling in infinite love and delight. It is mentioned as a
fit representation of that holy love which is said to be
like the precious ointment on the head that ran down
upon the beard, even Aaron's beard, that went down to
the skirts of his garments. It was from the fruit of the
olive tree, which it is known has been made use of as a
symbol of love or peace, which was probably taken from
the olive branch brought by the dove to Noah in token
of the divine favor; so that the olive branch and the
dove that brought it both signified the same thing,
love, which is specially typified by the precious oil from
the olive tree.

God's love is primarily to Himself, and His infinite
delight is in Himself, in the Father and the Son loving
and delighting in each other. We often read of the
Father loving the Son and being well-pleased in the
Son, and of the Son loving the Father. In the infinite
love and delight that is between these two Persons consists the infinite happiness of God. Proverbs 8:30:
"Then I was by him, as one brought up with him; and I
was daily his delight, rejoicing always before him." And
therefore, seeing that the Scripture signifies that the

Spirit of God is the Love of God, it follows that the Holy Spirit proceeds from or is breathed forth from the Father and the Son in some way or other infinitely above all our conceptions, as the divine essence entirely flows out and is breathed forth in infinitely pure love and sweet delight from the Father and the Son. This is that pure river of water of life that proceeds out of the throne of the Father and the Son, as we read at the beginning of Revelation 22; for Christ Himself tells us that by the water of life, or living water, is meant the Holy Ghost (John 7:38–39). This river of the water of life in Revelation is evidently the same with the living waters of the sanctuary in Ezekiel (Ezekiel 47:1ff.); and this river is doubtless the river of God's pleasure, or of God's own infinite delight spoken of in Psalm 36:7–9: "How excellent is Thy lovingkindness, O God! Therefore the children of men put their trust under the shadow of Thy wings. They shall be abundantly satisfied with the fatness of Thy house; and Thou shalt make them drink of the river of Thy pleasures. For with Thee is the fountain of life." The river of God's pleasures here spoken of is the same with the fountain of life spoken of in the next words. Here, as was observed before, the water of life, by Christ's own interpretation, is the Holy Spirit. This river of God's pleasures is also the same with the fatness of God's house, the holy oil of the sanctuary spoken of in the next preceding words, and is the same with God's love, or God's excellent loving-kindness, spoken of in the next preceding verse.

I have before observed that the Scripture abundantly reveals that the way in which Christ dwells in the saint is by His Spirit's dwelling in them. Here I would observe that Christ, in His prayer in John 17, seems to speak of the way in which He dwells in them as by the indwelling of the love wherewith the Father has loved Him. John 17:26: "And I have declared unto them Thy name, and will declare it; that the love wherewith Thou hast loved Me may be in them, and I in them." The beloved disciple who wrote this gospel had taken such particular notice of this that he afterwards, in his first epistle, once and again speaks of love's dwelling in the saints and the Spirit's dwelling in them being the same thing.

Again, the Scripture seems in many places to speak of love in Christians as if it were the same with the Spirit of God in them, or at least as the prime and most natural breathing and acting of the Spirit in the soul. So Romans 5:5: "Because the love of God is shed abroad in our hearts by the Holy Ghost, which is given unto us." Colossians 1:8: "Who also declared unto us your love in the Spirit." 2 Corinthians 6:6: "By kindness, by the Holy Ghost, by love unfeigned." Philippians 2:1: "If there be therefore any consolation in Christ, if any comfort of love, if any fellowship of the Spirit, if any bowels and mercies, fulfill ye my joy, that ye be like-minded, having the same love, being of one accord, of one mind."

The Scripture therefore leads us to this conclusion (though it is infinitely above us to conceive how it should be): that as the Son of God is the personal word, idea, or wisdom of God, begotten by God, being an infinitely perfect, substantial image or idea of Himself (as might be very plainly proven from the Holy Scripture, if here were the proper occasion for it), so the Holy Spirit does, in some ineffable and inconceivable manner, proceed, and is breathed forth both from the Father and the Son, by the divine essence being wholly poured and flowing out in that infinitely intense, holy, and pure love and delight that continually and unchangeably breathes forth from the Father and the Son, primarily towards each other, and secondarily towards the creature, and so flows forth in a different subsistence or person in a manner to us utterly inexplicable and inconceivable, and that this is that Person that is poured forth into the hearts of angels and saints.

Hence it is to be accounted for that, though we often read in Scripture of the Father loving the Son and the Son loving the Father, yet we never once read either of the Father or the Son loving the Holy Spirit, and the Spirit loving either of them. It is because the Holy Spirit is the divine love itself, the love of the Father and the Son. Hence also it is to be accounted for that we very often read of the love of both the Father and the Son to men, and particularly their love to the saints, but we never read of the Holy Ghost loving them, for the Holy Ghost is that love of God and Christ that is breathed forth primarily towards each other, and flows out secondarily towards the creature. This also will well account for it that the Apostle Paul so often wishes grace, mercy, and peace from God the Father, and from the Lord Jesus Christ, in the beginning of his epistles, without even mentioning the Holy Ghost, because the Holy Ghost is Himself the love and grace of God the Father and the Lord Jesus Christ. He is the Deity wholly breathed forth in infinite, substantial, intelligent love; from the Father and Son first towards each other, and secondarily freely flowing out to the creature, and so standing forth as a distinct personal subsistence.

Both the holiness and happiness of the Godhead

consists in this love. As we have already proven, all creature holiness consists essentially and summarily in love
to God and love to other creatures; so the holiness of
God consists in His love, especially in the perfect and
intimate union and love there is between the Father
and the Son. But the Spirit that proceeds from the
Father and the Son is the bond of this union, as it is of
all holy union between the Father and the Son, between God and the creature, and between the creatures
among themselves. All seems to be signified in Christ's
prayer in John 17 from verse 21 on. Therefore this Spirit
of love is the "bond of perfectness" (Colossians 3:14)
throughout the whole blessed society or family in
heaven and earth, consisting of the Father, the Head of
the family, and the Son, and all His saints who are the
disciples, seed, and spouse of the Son. The happiness of
God also consists in this love, for doubtless the happiness of God consists in the infinite love He has for
Himself and the delight He has in Himself, or, in other
words, in the infinite delight there is between the
Father and the Son, spoken of in Proverbs 8:30. This delight that the Father and the Son have in each other is
not to be distinguished from their love of complacence
one in another, wherein love most essentially consists,
as was observed before. The happiness of the Deity, as
all other true happiness, consists in love and society.

Hence it is that the Spirit of God, the third Person
in the Trinity, is so often called the Holy Spirit, as
though "Holy" were an epithet in some way or other
peculiarly belonging to Him, which can be no other
way than that the holiness of God consists in Him. He
is not only infinitely holy as the Father and the Son are,
but He is the holiness of God itself in the abstract. The

holiness of the Father and the Son consists in breathing forth this Spirit. Therefore He is not only called the Holy Spirit, but the Spirit of holiness. Romans 1:4: "According to the Spirit of holiness."

Hence also the river of "living waters," or the waters of life, which Christ explains in John 7 to mean the Holy Spirit, is, in the forementioned Psalm (36:8) called the "river of God's pleasures." Hence also that holy oil with which Christ was anointed, which I have shown was the Holy Ghost, is called the "oil of gladness." Hebrews 1:9: "Therefore God, even thy God, hath anointed thee with the oil of gladness above thy fellows." Hence we learn that God's fullness consists in the Holy Spirit. By "fullness," as the term is used in Scripture, as may easily be seen by looking over the texts that mention it, is intended the good that any one possesses. Now the good that God possesses most immediately consists in His joy and complacence that He has in Himself. It objectively, indeed, consists in the Father and the Son; but it most immediately consists in the complacence in these elements. Nevertheless the fullness of God consists in the holiness and happiness of the Deity. Hence persons, by being made partakers of the Holy Spirit, or having it dwelling in them, are said to be "partakers of the fullness of God" or Christ. Christ's fullness, as Mediator, consists in His having the Spirit given Him "not by measure" (John 3:34). And so it is that He is said to have "the fullness of the Godhead," which is said "to dwell in Him bodily (Colossians 2:9). We, by receiving the Holy Spirit from Christ and being made partakers of His Spirit, are said to "receive of His fullness, and grace for grace." And because this Spirit, which is the fullness of God, consists in the love of God and Christ, therefore we, by knowing the love of Christ, are said to "be filled with all the fullness of God" (Ephesians 3:19). For the way that we know the love of Christ is by having that love dwelling in us (1 John 4:13), because the fullness of God consists in the Holy Spirit. Hence our communion with God the Father and God the Son consists in our possessing the Holy Ghost, which is their Spirit. For to have communion or fellowship with either is to partake with them of their good in their fullness in union and society with them. Hence it is that we read of the saints having fellowship and communion with the Father and with the Son, but never of their having fellowship with the Holy Ghost, because the Holy Ghost is that common good or fullness which they partake of, in which their fellowship consists. We read of the communion of the Holy Ghost, but not of communion with Him, which are two very different things.

Persons are said to have communion with each other when they partake with each other in some common good; but any one is said to have communion of anything, with respect to that thing they partake of, in common with others. Hence, in the apostolic benediction, he wishes the "grace of the Lord Jesus Christ, and the love of God the Father, and the communion or partaking of the Holy Ghost." The blessing wished is but one: the Holy Spirit. To partake of the Holy Ghost is to have that love of the Father and the grace of the Son.

From what has been said, it follows that the Holy Spirit is the sum of all good. He is the fullness of God. The holiness and happiness of the Godhead consists in Him; and in communion or partaking of Him consists all the true loveliness and happiness of the creature. All the grace and comfort that persons here have, and all their holiness and happiness hereafter, consists in the love of the Spirit, spoken of in Romans 15:30, and joy in the Holy Ghost, spoken of in Romans 14:17; Acts 9:31 and 13:52. And therefore Matthew 7:11 says, "If ye then, being evil, know how to give good gifts unto your children, how much more shall your heavenly Father which is in heaven give good things to them that ask Him?" It is expressed thus in Luke 11:13: "If ye then, being evil, know how to give good gifts unto your children, how much more shall your Father give the Holy Spirit to them that ask Him?" Doubtless there is an agreement in what is expressed by each Evangelist; and giving the Holy Spirit to them who ask is the same as giving good things to them who ask, for the Holy Spirit is the sum of all good.

Hence we may better understand the economy of the Persons of the Trinity as it appears in the part that each one has in the affair of redemption, and shows the equality of each Person concerned in that affair, and the equality of honor and praise due to each of them. For that work, glory belongs to the Father and the Son, that they so greatly loved the world; to the Father, that He so loved the world that He gave His only-begotten Son, who was all His delight, who is His infinite, objective happiness; to the Son, that He so loved the world that He gave Himself. But there is equal glory due to the Holy Ghost on this account, because He is the love of the Father and the Son, that flows out primarily towards God and secondarily towards the elect whom Christ came to save. So that, however wonderful the love of the Father and the Son appear to be, so much the more glory belongs to the Holy Spirit, in whom subsists that wonderful and excellent love.

It shows the infinite excellency of the Father thus: that the Son so delighted in Him, and prized His honor and glory, that when He had a mind to save sinners, He came infinitely low, rather than men's salvation should be the injury of that honor and glory. It showed the infinite excellency and worth of the Son that the Father so delighted in Him that, for His sake, He was ready to quit His own; yea, and receive into favor those who had deserved infinite ill at His hands. Both show the infinite excellency of the Holy Spirit, because He is that delight of the Father and the Son in each other, which is manifested to be so great and infinite by these things.

What has been said shows that our dependence is equally on each Person in this affair. The Father approves and provides the Redeemer, and Himself accepts the price of the good purchased, and bestows that good. The Son is the Redeemer, and the price that is offered for the purchased good. And the Holy Ghost is the good purchased, for the sacred Scriptures seem to intimate that the Holy Spirit is the sum of all that Christ purchased for man (Galatians 3:13–14).

What Christ purchased for us is that we might have communion with God in His good, which consists in partaking or having communion of the Holy Ghost, as I have shown. All the blessedness of the redeemed consists in partaking of the fullness of Christ, their Head and Redeemer, which, I have observed, consists in partaking of the Spirit that is given Him not by measure. This is the vital sap which the creatures derive from the true vine. This is the holy oil poured on the Head that goes down to the members. Christ purchased for us that we should enjoy the love; but the love of God flows out in the proceeding of the Spirit, and He purchased for them that the love and joy of God should dwell in them, which is by the indwelling of the Holy Spirit.

The sum of all spiritual good which the saints have in this world is that spring of living water within them, which we read of in John 4:10, and those rivers of living waters flowing from within them, which we read of in John 7:38–39, which we are there told is the Holy Spirit. And the sum of all happiness in the other world is that river of living water which flows from the throne of God and the Lamb, which is the river of God's pleasures, and is the Holy Spirit, which is often compared in sacred Scripture to water, to the rain and dew, and rivers and floods of waters (Isaiah 44:3; 32:15; 41:17–18, [compared with John 4:14]; Isaiah 35:6–7 and 43:19–20).

The Holy Spirit is the purchased possession and inheritance of the saints, as appears because that little of it which the saints have in this world is said to be the earnest of that purchased inheritance (Ephesians 1:13–14; 2 Corinthians 1:22, 5:5). It is an earnest of that which we are to have a fullness of hereafter. The Holy Ghost is the great subject of all gospel promises, and therefore is called the Spirit of promise (Ephesians 1:13). He is called the promise of the Father (Luke 24:49).

The Holy Ghost being a comprehension of all good things promised in the gospel, we may easily see the force of the apostle's inquiry in Galatians 3:2: "This only would I know, received ye the Spirit by the works of the Law, or by the hearing of faith?" So that in the offer of redemption, it is of God of whom our good is purchased, and it is God who purchases it, and it is God also that is the thing purchased. Thus all our good

things are of God, through God, and in God. Romans
11:36: "For of Him, and through Him, and to Him, and
in Him (as the Greek *eis* is rendered in 1 Corinthians
8:6), are all things; to whom be glory forever." All our
good is of God the Father, and through God the Son,
and all is in the Holy Ghost, as He is Himself all our
good. So God is Himself the portion and purchased inheritance of His people. Thus God is the Alpha and
Omega in this affair of redemption.

If we suppose no more than used to be supposed
about the Holy Ghost, the honor of the Holy Ghost in
the work of redemption is not equal in any sense to the
Father and the Son's; nor is there an equal part of the
glory of this work belonging to Him. Merely to apply to
us, or immediately to give or hand to us a blessing purchased after it is purchased is subordinate to the other
two Persons, is but a little thing to the purchaser of it
by paying an infinite price by Christ, by Christ's offering up Himself a sacrifice to procure it. And it is but a
little thing to God the Father's giving His infinitely
dear Son to be a sacrifice for us to procure this good.
But according to what has now been supposed, there is
an equality. To be the wonderful love of God is as much
as for the Father and the Son to exercise wonderful
love; and to be the thing purchased is as much as to be
the price that purchased it. The price, and the thing
bought with that price, answer each other in value; and
to be the excellent benefit offered is as much as to offer
such an excellent benefit. For the glory that belongs to
Him who bestows the gospel arises from the excellency
and value of the gift, and therefore the glory is equal to
that excellency of the benefit. And so that Person who
is that excellent benefit has equal glory with Him who

bestows such an excellent benefit.

But now to return: from what has been now observed from the Holy Scriptures of the nature of the Holy Spirit, it may be clearly understood why grace in the hearts of the saints is called spiritual, in distinction from other things that are the effects of the Spirit in the hearts of men. For by this it appears that the divine principle in the saints is of the nature of the Spirit; for as the nature of the Spirit of God is divine love, so divine love is the nature and essence of that holy principle in the hearts of the saints.

The Spirit of God may operate and produce effects upon the minds of natural men who have no grace, as He does when He assists natural conscience and convictions of sin and danger. The Spirit of God may produce effects upon inanimate things, as of old He moved on the face of the waters. But He communicates holiness in His own proper nature only in those holy effects in the hearts of the saints. And, therefore, those holy effects only are called spiritual, and the saints only are called spiritual persons in sacred Scripture.

Men's natural faculties and principles may be assisted by the operation of the Spirit of God on their minds, to enable them to exert those acts which, to a greater or lesser degree, they exert naturally. But the Spirit doesn't at all communicate Himself in it in His own nature, which is divine love, any more than when He moved upon the face of the waters.

Hence also we may more easily receive and understand a doctrine that seems to be taught us in the sacred Scripture concerning grace in the heart, that it is no other than the Spirit of God itself dwelling and acting in the heart of a saint, which the consideration of these things will make manifest:

• The sacred Scriptures don't only call grace "spiritual," but "spirit."

• When the sacred Scriptures call grace "spirit," the Spirit of God is intended; and that grace is called "Spirit" no otherwise than as the name of the Holy Ghost, the third Person in the Trinity, is ascribed to it.

This holy principle is often called by the name of "spirit" in sacred Scripture. So John 3:6: "That which is born of the Spirit is spirit." Here, by "flesh" and "spirit," we have already shown, are intended those two opposite principles in the heart, corruption and grace. So by flesh and spirit the same things are manifestly intended in Galatians 5:17: "For the flesh lusteth against the spirit, and the spirit against the flesh; and these are contrary the one to the other; so that ye cannot do the things that ye would." This that is here given as the reason why Christians cannot do the things that they would is manifestly the same that is given for the same thing in the latter part of Romans 7. The reason there given why they cannot do the things that they would is that the law of the members war with and against the law of the mind; and therefore, by the law of the members and the law of the mind are meant the same as the flesh and spirit in Galatians. Yea, they are called by the same name of the flesh and spirit there, in that context, in the continuation of the same discourse in the beginning of the next chapter. "Therefore there is now no condemnation to them that are in Christ Jesus, that walk not after the flesh, but after the Spirit." Here the apostle evidently refers to the same two opposite principles warring one against another that he had been speaking of in the close of the preceding chapter, which he here calls flesh and spirit as he does in his epistle to the Galatians.

This is yet more abundantly clear by the next words, which are: "For the law of the spirit of life in Christ Jesus hath made me free from the law of sin and death." Here these two things, that in the preceding verse are called "flesh and spirit" are in this verse called "the law of the spirit of life" and "the law of sin and death," evidently speaking still of the same law of our mind and the law of sin spoken of in the last verse of the preceding chapter. The apostle goes on in Romans 8 to call estrangement and grace by the names of flesh and spirit (verses 4–9, and again verses 12–13). These two principles are called by the same names in Matthew 26:41: "The spirit indeed is willing, but the flesh is weak." There can be no doubt but that the same thing is intended here by the flesh and spirit as (compare what is said of the flesh and spirit here and in these places) in Romans 7–8 and Galatians 5. Again, these two principles are called by the same words in Galatians 6:8. If these are compared with Galatians 5:18, and with Romans 8:6 and 13, none can doubt but the same is meant in each place.

If the sacred Scriptures are duly observed, where grace is called by the name of "spirit," it will appear that it is so called by an ascription of the Holy Ghost, even the third Person in the Trinity, to that divine principle in the heart of the saints, as though that principle in them were no other than the Spirit of God itself, united to the soul, living and acting in it, and exerting itself in the use and improvement of its faculties.

Thus it is in Romans 8, as manifestly appears from verses 9–16: "But you are not in the flesh, but in the

Spirit, if so be the Spirit of God dwell in you. Now, if any man have not the Spirit of Christ, he is none of His." Here the apostle fully explains himself what he means when he so often calls that holy principle that is in the hearts of the saints by the name "spirit." He means this: the Spirit of God Himself dwelling and acting in them. In verse 9 he calls Him "the Spirit of God," and "the Spirit of Christ" in verse 10. He calls Him "Christ in you" in verse 11 and "the Spirit of Him who raised up Jesus from the dead" dwelling in them; and in verse 14 he calls Him "the Spirit of God." In verse 16 he calls Him "the Spirit itself." So He is called the Spirit of God in 1 Corinthians 2:11–12. So that that holy, divine principle which, we have observed, radically and essentially consists in divine love, is no other than a communication and participation of that same infinite, divine love which is God, and in which the Godhead is eternally breathed forth, and subsists in the third Person in the blessed Trinity. So that true, saving grace is no other than that very love of God, that is, God, in one of the Persons of the Trinity, uniting Himself to the soul of a creature as a vital principle, dwelling there and exerting Himself by the faculties of the soul of man, in His own proper nature, after the manner of a principle of nature.

And we may look back and more fully understand what the Apostle John means when he says once and again, "God is Love," and "He that dwelleth in love dwelleth in God, and God in him," and "If we love one another, God dwelleth in us," and "His love is perfected in us," and "Hereby we know that we dwell in Him and He in us, because He has given us of His Spirit."

By this also we may understand what the Apostle

Peter means in 2 Peter 1:4, when he says that the saints are made "partakers of the divine nature." They are not only partakers of a nature that may, in some sense, be called divine because it is conformed to the nature of God, but the very Deity does, in some sense, dwell in them. That holy and divine love dwells in their hearts, and is so united to human faculties, that it has itself become a principle of new nature. That love which is the very native tongue and spirit of God so dwells in their souls that He exerts Himself in His own nature in the exercise of those faculties, after the manner of a natural or vital principle in them.

This shows us how the saints are said to be the "temples of the Holy Ghost" (as they are in 1 Corinthians 3:16–17; 6:19; 2 Corinthians 6:16). By this, also, we may understand how the saints are said to be made partakers of God's holiness, not only as they partake of holiness that God gives, but partake of that holiness by which He Himself is holy. For it has been already observed that the holiness of God consists in that divine love in which the essence of God really flows out.

This also shows us how to understand our Lord when He speaks of His joy being fulfilled in the saints. John 17:13: "And now I come unto thee; and these things I speak in the world, that they might have My joy fulfilled in themselves." It is by the indwelling of that divine Spirit, which we have shown to be God the Father's and the Son's infinite love and joy in each other. In verse 13 He says that He has spoken His word to His disciples that His joy might be fulfilled; and in verse 26 He says, "And I have declared unto them Thy name, and will declare it; that the love wherewith Thou hast loved Me may be in them, and I in them."

And herein lies the mystery of the vital union that is between Christ and the soul of a believer, which orthodox divines speak so much of, Christ's love; that is, His Spirit is actually united to the faculties of their souls. So He properly lives, acts, and exerts His nature in the exercise of their faculties. By this love being in them, He is in them (John 17:26); and so it is said in 1 Corinthians 6:17: "But he that is joined to the Lord is one spirit."

And thus it is that the saints are said to live, yet not they, but Christ lives in them (Galatians 2:20). The very promise of spiritual life in their souls is no other than the Spirit of Christ Himself. So that they live by His life as much as the members of the body live by the life of the Lord, and as much as the branches live by the life of the root and stock. "Because I live, ye shall live also" (John 14:19). "We are dead; but our life is hid with Christ in God" (Colossians 3:3). "When Christ, who is our life, shall appear. . ." (Colossians 3:4).

There is a union with Christ by the indwelling of the love of Christ in two ways: first, as it is from Christ, and is the very Spirit and life and fullness of Christ; and second, as it acts to Christ; for the very nature of it is love and union of heart to Him.

Because the Spirit of God dwells as a vital principle or a principle of new life in the soul, therefore He is called the "Spirit of life" (Romans 8:2), and the Spirit that quickens (John 6:63).

The Spirit of God is a vital principle in the soul, as the breath of life is in the body. Ezekiel 37:5: "Thus saith the Lord God unto these bones, 'I will cause breath to enter into you, and ye shall live,' " and so verses 9–10.

That principle of grace that is in the hearts of the saints is as much a proper communication or participation of the Spirit of God, the third Person in the Trinity, as that breath that entered into these bodies is represented to be a participation of the wind that blew upon them. The prophet says, "Come from the four winds, O breath, and breathe upon these slain that they may live," and that is now the very same wind and the same breath, but only was lacking to these bodies to be a vital principle in them, which otherwise would be dead. And therefore Christ Himself represents the communication of His Spirit to His disciples by His breathing upon them, and communicating to them His breath (John 20:22).

We often, in our common language about things of this nature, speak of a principle of grace. I suppose there is no other principle of grace in the soul than the very Holy Ghost dwelling in the soul and acting there as a vital principle. To speak of a habit of grace as a natural disposition to act grace, as begotten in the soul by the first communication of Divine light, and as the natural and necessary consequence of the first light, it seems in some respects to carry a wrong idea with it. Indeed the first exercise of grace in the first light has a tendency to future acts, as from an abiding principle, by grace and by the covenant of God, but not by any natural force. Giving one gracious discovery or act of grace, or a thousand, has no proper natural tendency to cause an abiding habit of grace for the future, nor any otherwise than by divine constitution and covenant. But all succeeding acts of grace must be as immediately and, to all intents and purposes, as much from the immediate acting of the Spirit of God on the soul as the

first; and if God should take away His Spirit out of the
soul, all habits and acts of grace would of themselves
cease as immediately as light ceases in a room when a
candle is carried out. And no man has a habit of grace
dwelling in him any otherwise than as he has the Holy
Spirit dwelling in him in his temple, and acting in
union with his natural faculties, after the manner of a
vital principle. So that when they act grace, it is, in the
language of the apostle, not they, but Christ living in
them. Indeed the Spirit of God, united to human faculties, acts very much after the manner of a natural principle or habit. So that one act makes way for another,
and so it now settles the soul in a disposition to holy
acts—but that it does so as by grace and covenant, and
not from any natural necessity.

Hence the Spirit of God seems in sacred Scripture to
be spoken of as a quality of the persons in whom it
resided. So that they are called spiritual persons; and
when we say a virtuous man, we speak of virtue as the
quality of the man. It is the Spirit itself that is the only
principle of true virtue in the heart. So that to be truly
virtuous is the same as to be spiritual.

And thus it is not only with respect to the virtue that
is in the hearts of the saints on earth, but also the perfect virtue and holiness of the saints in heaven. It consists altogether in the indwelling and acting of the
Spirit of God in their habits. And so it was with man before the fall; and so it is with elect, sinless angels. We
have shown that the holiness and happiness of God
consist in the Holy Spirit; and so the holiness and happiness of every holy or truly virtuous creature of God, in
heaven or earth, consist in the communion of the same
Spirit.